Estate Planning
for the
Savvy Client

WHAT YOU NEED TO KNOW BEFORE
YOU MEET WITH YOUR LAWYER

Mary L. Barrow, Esq.

Savvy Client Press

620 Park Avenue, Ste. 242

Rochester, New York 14607

info@savvyclientpress.com

Ordering Information:

Quantity sales. Special discounts are available on quantity purchases by corporations, associations, and others. For details, contact the address above.

Estate Planning for the Savvy Client/ Mary L. Barrow. —1st ed.

ISBN 978-0692853061

This book is a brief summary only and should not be used as a substitute for the advice of competent legal counsel from an attorney admitted or authorized to practice law in your jurisdiction. You should always consult your attorney before implementing or changing any estate planning strategy. You should never delay seeking legal advice, disregard legal advice, or commence or discontinue any legal action because of information in this book.

Contents

About the Author...1

Introduction..3

   Why I Wrote This Book............................4

   What This Book Is.....................................5

   What This Book Is Not..............................5

Basics You'll Want to Know...........................7

   What Is Estate Planning?..........................8

   What Does "Property" Really Mean?...................8

   Other Terms You Should Know 9

   What Does a Typical Estate Plan Include?...........9

   What Happens if You Don't Have an Estate Plan?
....10

   What Is Probate? 11

   What to Expect When You Meet With Your
Attorney 13

The Number One Misconception About Wills.....17

   What a Will Does....................................18

Some Property Does Not Pass by Will 18

Property That Passes by Beneficiary Designation
.... 19

Property That Passes by Law 20

Property That Passes by Will 22

Spousal and Contractual Rights and the Like 22

Let's Illustrate These Concepts 23

Probate Property and Non-Probate Property 24

An Estate Plan Is Like a Puzzle 25

More About Wills You'll Want to Know 29

What Happens to Your Property if You Don't
Have a Will? 29

What Your Will Should Include 31

Where Should You Keep Your Will? 38

You Need a Will Even if You Think You Don't 39

What Happens if You Become Incapacitated? 43

What Happens Without Prior Planning? 43

"Putting Someone's Name" on Your Accounts ..44

Using a Power of Attorney for Finances 46

Making Your Healthcare Wishes Known 52

Do You Need a Trust? 55

What Exactly Is a Trust? 55

Why You May Want a Trust 57

Two Types of Trusts 59

How a Trust Is Created 60

How a Trust Is Funded 60

What Does a Trustee Do? 61

Who Should You Name as Your Trustee? 62

Revocable Living Trusts 65

What Is a Revocable Living Trust? 65

Do You Need a Revocable Living Trust? 66

Why Avoid Probate? 67

Using a Revocable Living Trust to Avoid Probate

.... 73

Using a Revocable Living Trust in Case of

Incapacity 76

Working With an Attorney 81

Why You Need an Attorney 81

How to Choose an Attorney 84

Keeping Your Estate Plan Up to Date 90

Conclusion 95

Index 97

This book is dedicated to all of my clients and students over the years.
You are the joy of my practice.

"Everything should be made as simple as possible, but not simpler."

Albert Einstein

About the Author

Mary L. Barrow has been an attorney for more than 30 years. She has a BA from Brown University and a JD from the University of Pennsylvania law school. For many years she practiced estate planning, probate and trust law, in three different states, both as a partner in a large law firm and as the principal of a boutique trusts & estates firm. She has helped numerous clients define their goals and objectives, and then implement those wishes as simply and efficiently as possible through their estate plans.

In 2009 Attorney Barrow was approached by the Osher Lifelong Learning Institute (OLLI) at the University of South Carolina Beaufort to create a course for its members on the topic of trusts. She was delighted to teach the resulting course for a number of years. Attorney Barrow enjoys speaking to groups of non-lawyers on estate planning topics.

Introduction

Welcome to *Estate Planning For the Savvy Client*. This book is your guide to getting the most out of your relationship with your estate planning lawyer.

A quick search of any online or brick-and-mortar bookstore will tell you that there are already many trusts & estates books in the world. They cover wills, trusts, probate, and a variety of other estate planning topics. There are do-it-yourself books and technical "let's-learn-everything-from-a-book" books. There are guides and templates and checklists. There are in-depth analyses written by experts in the field. But when it comes to planning your own estate, no matter how many books you may read, unless you have a law degree and years of experience practicing trusts & estates law, you'll benefit greatly from the guidance of a qualified trusts & estates attorney. In the pages that follow, I draw on my extensive experience to help you get as much as you can from your lawyer's time.

Why I Wrote This Book

When I taught a course on trusts for the Osher Lifelong Learning Institute (OLLI), I found that many of my students were sophisticated, successful people who had already met with an attorney and obtained estate planning documents, such as wills, trusts, and powers of attorney. But they came to my course because they still had questions or concerns. I understand how this could happen: In the first place, trusts & estates is a highly technical, detail-oriented area of the law. There often simply is not enough time to address all the fine points. Second, people are sometimes reluctant to ask questions that they feel are either too basic (and therefore embarrassing) or too complex. In addition, there is a mindset and a vocabulary in the world of estate planning, probate and trust law that is second nature to the people who work in that system. Lawyers and other people working within the system may assume that people understand certain terms and procedures when that simply is not the case.

I wrote this book so that the money you spend on estate planning is money well spent. I'll explain some basic concepts and dispel some common estate planning myths and misconceptions so that you can be better-informed and more self-confident before you consult a prospective lawyer or meet with your current lawyer. I'll also help you close any communication gaps that may exist between you and your lawyer. Better communication between you and your lawyer will make it easier to achieve your estate planning goals and objectives efficiently.

Did You Know? It is unlikely that all your assets will pass as specified in your Last Will and Testament. Read Chapter 2.

Did You Know? "Putting your daughter's name" on a bank account or putting your house "in your son's name" could have serious adverse consequences. Read Chapter 4.

What This Book Is

This book is designed to make you more comfortable with the estate planning process. It will give you insight into what to expect and explain important terms and concepts. We'll start with the basics and move on to more advanced concepts. Understanding these fundamentals will help you make the most of your time, energy and money when planning your estate, as well as give you more confidence.

Whether you are new to estate planning or making changes to your existing plan, you'll benefit from reading this book before your next meeting with your attorney. The Savvy Client is you!

What This Book Is Not

This book is not legal advice and it isn't a substitute for legal advice from a qualified estate planning attorney and/or tax advisor. It provides a general overview of selected trusts & estates concepts in the United States of America. Keep in mind that specific laws and practices differ in each of the fifty states. Moreover, the information in this book may not apply to your specific situation. You should always consult an experienced estate planning attorney and/or tax advisor for legal or tax advice on your local laws and unique circumstances.

After reading this book, you will have a greater understanding and be better prepared to work with your lawyer, but you won't be qualified to plan your own estate or draft your own estate planning documents any more than you would be qualified to remove your own gall bladder after reading a book on surgery. And you won't know more than your attorney (if you suspect you do, get a different attorney).

Finally, reading this book is not intended to and does not create an attorney-client relationship between us, and the book is not a solicitation for legal work.

CHAPTER 1

Basics You'll Want to Know

You'll be much more comfortable with the estate planning process if you have a solid understanding of some of the basic concepts. I remember (although it was many years ago) being perplexed the first time I heard the term "estate planning." What was that, exactly? What do we mean by an "estate plan"? Is it a single piece of paper with a plan on it, or is it something altogether different? And how do we do whatever it is? This chapter will shed light on these and other murky areas.

Throughout this book, you'll see some terms in **bold** print. Those are terms that I will define in a general, traditional trusts & estates manner. Bear in mind that each state may have adopted different terms for the same concepts. For example, many states have replaced the traditional term "executor" with the term "personal representative." This should not interfere with your understanding of the general concepts.

What Is Estate Planning?

Generally speaking, your **estate** is all of the property you own at your death, both in your sole name and as a co-owner with others. Ideally, your **estate plan** is a plan that you devise (with the assistance of your attorney) long before your death so that, when you die, your assets go to the people you choose, and in the manner you want.

What Does "Property" Really Mean?

Although many people think of real estate when they hear the term "property," in the estate planning context, **property** means all of your assets, not just real estate. Property includes both **real property**, which is real estate, and **personal property**, which is everything else. Personal property includes **tangible personal property** and **intangible personal property**. Tangible personal property is personal property that you can touch, such as books, jewelry, clothing, furniture and so on. Intangible personal property is personal property that has no physical form, such as bank accounts, stocks, bonds, insurance, retirement accounts, annuities, business interests, and the like.

Property = Real Property + Personal Property

Real Property = Real Estate

Personal Property = Tangible Personal Property + Intangible Personal Property

Tangible Personal Property = Property That You Can Touch

Intangible Personal Property = Property That Has no Physical Form

Other Terms You Should Know

Leaving real property to someone under a Will is traditionally called a **devise**. For example, a Will might say, "I give and devise my real property located at 123 Main Street to Mary." Leaving someone personal property under a Will is traditionally called a **bequest**. For example, a Will might say, "I give and bequeath my silver tea service to Eileen." The person receiving the property is typically called the **beneficiary**.

In estate planning, the deceased person is often called the **decedent** (də-cé-dənt), and in the case of a married couple, the spouse of a decedent is called the **surviving spouse**.

You may also hear the terms probate estate and taxable estate. Your **probate estate** is the portion of your assets subject to the probate process (which we will discuss shortly). Your **taxable estate** is the portion of your assets which may be subject to federal or state estate or inheritance taxes.

What Does a Typical Estate Plan Include?

A basic estate plan typically includes:

- a Will, also known as a Last Will and Testament,

- health care directive(s), such as an Advance Directive, Living Will, and/or Health Care Power of Attorney, and
- a power of attorney relating to the management of your assets.

An estate plan might also include a revocable living trust, also known as an intervivos trust. This type of trust is sometimes called a "Will substitute" because it can take the place of a Will in determining how assets pass at death.

> *Estate Plan =*   *Last Will and Testament ("Will")*
> *Revocable Living Trust (optional)*
> *Power of Attorney for finances*
> *Health Care Directives*

Estate planning can also include many other techniques for many different purposes. These other techniques are beyond the scope of this book, which will discuss the basic elements of an estate plan.

What Happens if You Don't Have an Estate Plan?

If you don't have an estate plan, your property certainly will still be transferred to someone, but it may not be to the person or in the manner you would have wanted. If you don't have a Will, state law decides who gets your property and who will be in charge of settling your estate. If you have young children and don't have a Will that names guardians for them, a court will decide who will be their guardian without input from you.

For example, many married people want all of their assets to pass to their surviving spouse. However, without a Will, the law in some states provides instead that a portion of the assets must go directly to the deceased person's children.

Typically, estate planning also includes arrangements for managing your assets if you become physically or mentally incapable of handling matters on your own during your life. Without such planning, expensive and time-consuming legal proceedings, such as a guardianship, may be required.

Finally, your estate plan should include directions regarding your medical care, such as life support, in the event that you are unable to make your own decisions. If you don't make your health care wishes known in advance, it may be much harder on family members during what is already a difficult time.

What Is Probate?

Probate is a legal proceeding in which a deceased person's Will is submitted to a court (sometimes called a probate court) which has legal authority (**jurisdiction**) over the settlement of the deceased person's estate. The court determines whether or not the Will is valid and appoints an **executor** (sometimes called a "**personal representative**") to carry out the terms of the Will. There is usually ongoing court supervision of the progress of the estate administration.

For example, the executor must **account** for his or her actions. This typically means that the executor will have to submit paperwork to the court (an **accounting**) that shows:

- all of the assets in the estate as of the beginning of the estate administration (the date of death),
- any income earned by the assets during the period of the estate administration,
- any debts, expenses, and taxes paid during the estate administration, and
- the proposed amounts to be distributed to the beneficiaries.

In some jurisdictions the court itself will examine the accounting and approve or disapprove it. In other jurisdictions the court will only consider objections if someone else (for example, a beneficiary) brings them up.

A popular misconception is that probate must be avoided at all costs. But the reality is that *it depends*. Probate procedures vary enormously, not only from state to state, but even from court to court. You'll want to find out how your local probate court rates on the following factors:

- How high are the probate fees? In some parts of the country the fees your estate will have to pay to the court (probate fees) are very expensive and to be avoided. In other places, they are minimal and may not be worth the trouble of avoiding.
- Will the court process prolong the settlement of your estate? In some places it may take weeks, if not months, just to have your executor appointed. In other places, all the court needs is your original Will, your death certificate, and some simple paperwork, and it will appoint your executor the same day.

- How daunting is the paperwork? In some places, the probate forms are simple and in others they can appear incomprehensible.
- Does the probate process add value? You may feel that having a judge oversee what your executor is doing adds tremendous value in making sure that your wishes, as expressed in your Will, are followed. On the other hand, you may feel that the process is more bureaucratic in nature and adds little value.

Your attorney can help you find these answers and advise you regarding whether avoiding probate is desirable where you live. In **Chapter 6, *Revocable Living Trusts*,** I will discuss these factors in greater detail when we talk about avoiding probate by using a revocable living trust.

Many states have small estate proceedings designed to handle estates with a value less than a certain amount (typically some number around $25,000 -$40,000 or maybe more). If the probate assets are worth less than the specified amount, then the Will does not have to be probated. Rather, there is a simplified (and usually inexpensive) procedure that allows the probate assets to be distributed in accordance with the Will.

What to Expect When You Meet With Your Attorney

To help you plan your estate properly, your attorney will need to know what your assets are and how you want them to pass at your death. Typically, before your appointment your attorney will send you a questionnaire about your family and each asset that you own.

Even more important, your attorney needs to know *how* you own each asset. For example, do you own it in your sole name or with another person? Do you own it in a retirement account such as an IRA or 401(k)? With respect to real estate, how exactly is the ownership stated on the deed?

You'll probably have to do some homework to answer these questions, and it may seem like an annoyance, but it is crucial to your estate plan. Why? Because the legal form in which you own an asset determines how it passes at death. We'll discuss this in much more detail in **Chapter 2, *The Number One Misconception About Wills*.**

Typically, the next step will be meeting with your attorney to discuss your goals and objectives. It's okay if you're not clear about them yet; your attorney can help you define them. Your wishes should be the focus of the discussion. Everything about the estate plan should be designed to achieve your goals and objectives in the simplest and most efficient way possible.

Sometimes clients (and attorneys) want to start discussing specific estate planning techniques, such as types of trusts or other complex techniques that they may have heard about, without knowing how these techniques contribute to the achievement of their goals. That is the cart driving the horse–you should know why any technique is right for you specifically.

• *Remember*

If you're married with children and die without a Will, your surviving spouse might not inherit all of your assets.

The term "property" doesn't just mean real estate. In estate planning, "property" means <u>all</u> your assets, both real property (real estate) and personal property.

CHAPTER 2

The Number One Misconception About Wills

Thinking back, you remember that your attorney prepared a Will for you and that you signed it in front of witnesses. You took the Will home and put it in a file cabinet. You seem to remember that your Will says that when you die your estate will pass to your three children in equal shares. You can rest easy, knowing that when you die, all of your assets (after the payment of debts, expenses and taxes) will be divided into three equal shares and paid to your children. Seems like a reasonable assumption, right?

Not so fast. While in the not too distant past that may have been a reasonable assumption, in this day and age the reality is that it is unlikely that all of your property will be distributed in accordance with your Will. This chapter explains why and what you may want to do about it.

What a Will Does

A Will's most basic functions are:

- to specify how your estate shall be distributed at your death,
- to name your executor, who is the person who will be responsible for collecting, administering and distributing your estate in accordance with your Will, and
- if you have young children, to name a guardian for them.

A typical Will refers to "all property owned by me at my death" or "my property, both real and personal, of whatever kind and nature and wherever situated" or similar words. It would be natural, therefore, to assume that once you had finished making your Will, upon your death all of your property would be transferred according to its terms. For example, if your Will states that all of your property shall pass, in equal shares, to each of three people, it would be reasonable to assume that all of your property will be divided among those three people. After all, it sounds so definite and says "all my property" or something similar to that.

But it often doesn't work that way. In my experience, the number one misconception about Wills is the belief that all of your property will be distributed as your Will directs.

Some Property Does Not Pass by Will

If the number one misconception regarding Wills is that a Will transfers all your property, then what is the reality? The truth is that certain types of property do not pass by Will, and your Will has no effect on how such property passes upon your death.

This bears repeating: **Some Property Does Not Pass by Will**. Don't assume that all of your property will pass to the people named in your Will.

Property That Passes by Beneficiary Designation

Certain types of property, notably life insurance, IRAs, 401(k)s, annuities, pensions and the like, do not pass by Will. Rather they pass to a beneficiary you named on the account when you filled out something called a **beneficiary designation**. When you die, the property is transferred to the beneficiary named in the beneficiary designation regardless of what your Will says. In other words, the beneficiary designation overrides the Will.

Example

Your Will states that upon your death your entire estate passes to your three children, Tom, Dick and Harry, in equal shares. You have a $1,000,000 life insurance policy. The life insurance company's records show that the beneficiary of the policy is Tom. You die. The insurance company pays the entire $1,000,000 to Tom.

In many cases, you filled out the beneficiary designation many years ago or in a casual way and have long since forgotten about it. As part of the estate planning process it's a good idea to request, for each account that you own, a written statement of the beneficiaries from the insurance company or financial institution.

In addition to life insurance, IRAs, 401(k)s, annuities, pensions and the like, it's also now possible to name beneficiaries on financial accounts, by a method known as a POD (payable on death) or TOD (transfer on death) designation. You may have placed such a designation on all kinds of bank accounts and brokerage accounts when you opened the account or at any time after you opened the account. POD and TOD designations are fairly recent developments, so you may have beneficiaries on accounts which you would ordinarily not think of as having a beneficiary.

Property That Passes by Law

Certain types of property, notably property you own with another person, may pass by law and not by Will. For instance, some types of joint ownership mean that upon the death of one of the joint owners, the deceased person's share of the property passes automatically to the other joint owner(s) regardless of what the decedent's Will says. These types of ownership are usually, but not always, created when the property is first acquired, perhaps many years ago.

Keep an eye out for bank or brokerage accounts that may be owned jointly. Joint ownership is different from a POD or TOD designation, discussed above. You may need to go back to the financial institution's records-perhaps the original signature cards-to see how the account was legally opened. Do not confuse legal ownership with the mailing address on the account, which may have no legal significance. Read *"Putting Someone's Name" on Your Accounts* in **Chapter 4**, which discusses some of the consequences of joint ownership of bank accounts.

Deeds to real estate are particularly tricky. Even if you know that there are two people listed as the owners on a deed, you still won't know how the property passes upon the death of one of the owners without:

- further examining the deed, and
- knowing the law in the state where the real estate is located.

There are many ways for property to pass by deed depending on state law. Here are two of the main ways:

Joint tenancy with right of survivorship. The deceased person's share of the property passes automatically to the surviving owner(s) by law, regardless of what the deceased person's Will says.

Tenancy in common. The deceased person's share of the property passes according to his or her Will.

Example

We know from looking at a real estate deed that "Janet and Dean" own the property. But we still need more information. Do Janet and Dean own the property as "joint tenants with right of survivorship," or a similar designation? If so, then when Janet dies, her share of the property passes to Dean automatically by law, and vice versa. However, it could also be that Janet and Dean own the property as "tenants in common," or a similar designation, which means that when Janet dies, her share of the property passes by Will to the beneficiaries named in her Will, and vice versa.

So which is it? The answer is determined by the exact wording of the deed and by state law, which defines how the different types of joint ownership are created.

Property That Passes by Will

Now you can see why, even though your Will may say that "all" your property should be distributed in a certain way, that is unlikely to happen. Only property that does not pass by beneficiary designation or by law is subject to the provisions of your Will. Property that passes by Will is usually limited to such things as tangible personal property, real estate or bank accounts that are solely-owned and have no beneficiary designation.

Example

Tom owns a house and is named as the sole owner on the deed. He also owns a bank account and a brokerage account in his sole name. During his life, he does not create any other rights in any other person; that is, there is no joint owner or beneficiary for any of these assets. It appears that all of Tom's property passes by Will at his death.

Spousal and Contractual Rights and the Like

In this chapter we have explained that how you own your property, that is, the way you hold legal title, has a big impact on your estate plan. But we are not considering any legal rights that someone (other than a named co-owner or named beneficiary) may have to inherit something from your estate.

For example, if you are married, your surviving spouse may have the legal right to inherit a portion of your property, regardless of what your Will says. This is particularly true if you live in a community property state. Likewise, you may be contractually obligated to leave a portion of your estate to someone else, for example, under a separation agreement or divorce decree.

These and other situations could, of course, cause your property to be distributed other than as stated in your Will, but are beyond the scope of this book. You should be advised by your attorney as to whether a similar situation could apply to you.

Let's Illustrate These Concepts

The following quizzes illustrate the concepts discussed in this chapter. The answers appear at the end of the chapter.

Quiz #1

- Brenda has three children. Her Will provides that her estate is to be divided equally among them. Her primary assets are a house worth $300,000, a brokerage account worth $200,000, and a checking account worth $100,000. She has "put her daughter's name" on her checking account for convenience, so that the daughter may write checks and so forth.

- At her death, how does her estate pass?

- How do you think she wanted it to pass?

Quiz #2

- David gets a divorce and dies a few months later. His Will provides that his estate is to be evenly divided among his three children. David has a sizable 401(k) plan, the named beneficiary of which is still his ex-wife because he never got around to changing the beneficiary designation after his divorce.

- Who gets the proceeds of the 401(k)?

- How do you think he wanted it to pass?

Quiz #3

- Jane has been working at the same company for many years. Her employer provides the employees with group life insurance coverage. On Jane's first day of work, she filled out all the employee benefit forms and named her mother as the beneficiary of her life insurance. Since then, she has married and had three children. Her Will provides that her estate passes to her spouse.

- If Jane dies, who gets the proceeds of the life insurance?

- How do you think she wanted it to pass?

Probate Property and Non-Probate Property

As you plan your estate, you will want to keep in mind the difference between "probate" and "non-probate" property.

If you own property that passes by Will it is typically called **probate property** and the total of all your probate property is called your **probate estate**. A probate court process will be required in order for your probate property to be transferred to the people named in your Will. If you don't have any probate property, then your Will may not have to be probated (that is, you might "avoid probate").

If you own property that does not pass by Will, such as property that passes by beneficiary designation and property that passes by law, it is called **non-probate property**. In order for this kind of property to be transferred to your beneficiaries, there does not need to be a probate court process. For example, a life insurance company can pay the proceeds of a life insurance policy directly to your named beneficiary without court involvement.

An Estate Plan Is Like a Puzzle

In recent years there has been a proliferation of new, legally created methods for passing property at death by beneficiary designation and by law. While these methods are useful for some purposes, they make estate planning much more complicated because you can't simply assume that your property will pass in accordance with the provisions of your Will.

It's important, therefore, that as part of the estate planning process, you and your attorney know precisely how you own each asset. Otherwise, you can't be sure that all the pieces of your plan will fit together.

I have had clients tell me that they were positive that an asset (for example, a piece of real estate) was owned jointly, but then when I took a look at the paperwork (the deed) it was, in fact, owned solely, and vice versa.

It may take a bit of detective work to obtain the information required to make these determinations, but it is well worth the effort. Share the information with your attorney so that he or she can make sure that the legal consequences are what you think they are. You'll also want to have that information in your files when it comes time for your executor to settle your estate.

Answer to Quiz #1

It appears that Brenda's total estate is worth about $600,000 and that she wants it divided equally among her three children, so that each would receive property worth about $200,000.

However, when she "put her daughter's name" on her checking account she may have created a joint account with her daughter. That would mean that upon her death, the daughter would receive the entire $100,000 checking account.

The remaining $500,000 (house and brokerage account) would be the probate estate, which would be divided into thirds (roughly $166,667 each) in accordance with the Will.

Therefore the daughter would receive $266,667 (the $100,000 checking account plus her 1/3 of the probate estate), and each of the other two children would receive $166,667.

This is likely not the result Brenda wanted.

Moral of the story: Know the legal consequences of your actions. Let your attorney know how you own your assets and if you change the manner of ownership later.

Answer to Quiz #2

David's ex-wife receives the proceeds of his 401(k). His beneficiary designation overrides the Will. This is probably not what David wanted.

This example is based on a similar case that was decided by the United States Supreme Court in 2001. The Court decided that the beneficiary was entitled to the account despite the fact that the state in question had passed a law which said that, upon divorce, any beneficiary designations to the ex-spouse were null and void (*Egelhoff* v. *Egelhoff*, 121 S. Ct. 1322 (2001)).

Moral of the story: Make sure your beneficiary designations are up to date. Doing so should be as much a part of the estate planning process as writing a Will.

Answer to Quiz #3

Jane's mother receives the proceeds of the life insurance policy. Jane's beneficiary designation overrides the Will. This is probably not what Jane wanted. It's possible that she still wanted to leave the life insurance proceeds to her mother (and everything else to her spouse), but without an up-to-date beneficiary designation, we can't know for sure.

Moral of the story: Make sure your beneficiary designations are up to date. Doing so should be as much a part of the estate planning process as writing a Will.

- ## *Remember*

  The legal form in which you own an asset determines who gets it when you die. Check how you own your assets.

  ### *Real estate:*

  Who are the named owners on the deed?
  If more than one named owner, are they joint tenants, tenants in common, or something else?
  Does the deed specify a beneficiary?

  ### *Bank or brokerage accounts:*

  Who are the owners of the account?
  If more than one named owner, are they joint owners or something else?
  Is there a POD or TOD designation on the account?

  ### *Life insurance, IRAs, 401(k)s, annuities, pensions:*

  Who are the primary beneficiaries?
  Who are the secondary beneficiaries?

  ### *Vehicles:*

  Who are the named owners on the registration?
  If more than one, are they joint owners or something else?
  Does the registration specify a beneficiary?

CHAPTER 3

More About Wills You'll Want to Know

A Last Will and Testament ("**Will**") is a basic building block of an estate plan. In this chapter we'll look at the different parts a Will should have, why you need one, and where you should keep it.

What Happens to Your Property if You Don't Have a Will?

If you don't have a Will, then any property which would otherwise pass by Will (your probate estate) instead passes according to state law. These laws are generally called **intestacy laws** and this situation is typically referred to as an **intestacy** or an **intestate estate**.

The intestacy laws of your state determine which relatives inherit your probate estate if you don't have a valid Will. Such relatives are called your **legal heirs** (sometimes called distributees). In most cases your legal heirs will be your surviving spouse, your children, and any grandchildren of a deceased child, but this can vary in certain particulars from state to state. If at the time of your death you have no surviving spouse, children or grandchildren, then the law specifies how your estate will be divided among more remote relatives, such as surviving parents, siblings, nieces and nephews.

Examples

Michael lives in State A and dies without a Will. At the time of his death, he has a surviving spouse and three surviving children. His probate estate is valued at $100,000. The intestacy laws of State A say that if a deceased person is survived by a spouse and children, the spouse receives one-half of the estate and the other half is divided among the surviving children. His spouse will receive $50,000 and each of his children will receive about $16,667.

Assume the same facts as above, except that Michael lives in State B. The intestacy laws of State B say that the surviving spouse receives $50,000 off the top plus one-half of the rest of the estate, and the balance is divided among the surviving children. His spouse will receive $75,000 ($50,000 plus $25,000) and each of his children will receive about $8,334.

Lydia lives in State A and dies without a Will. At the time of her death, she has no surviving spouse, children or parents. Lydia has a surviving sister, who has three children. She also has a surviving niece and nephew, who are the children of Lydia's deceased brother. Her probate estate is valued at $100,000. The intestacy laws of State A say that one-half of Lydia's estate passes to her sister and the other half passes to the children of her deceased brother in equal shares. Lydia's sister will receive $50,000 and the children of her deceased brother will receive $25,000 each.

What Your Will Should Include

The primary purposes of your Will are to:

- give your instructions regarding your probate property,
- name your executor, and
- name a guardian for your minor children (if any).

Make sure your Will clearly states what should happen to all of the property in your probate estate so that state law doesn't make those decisions for you.

Your Tangible Personal Property

Typically, a Will contains a separate provision for the distribution of your tangible personal property. For example, "I give and bequeath all of my tangible personal property and household effects and the like wherever situated, such as jewelry, clothing, automobiles, furniture, furnishings, silver, crystal, china, books and pictures, to my spouse, John." As we saw in **Chapter 1**, *Basics You'll Want to Know*, tangible personal property is personal property (not real estate), that you can touch; for example, the items listed in the previous sentence. Such property is sometimes also known as your "personal effects."

Often the value of tangible personal property is more sentimental than economic, but not always. Make sure you specify not only who is to receive your tangible personal property but also, if there is more than one person, the method used to divide up the property. For example, "I give and bequeath my tangible personal property to my children who survive me, to be divided as they agree or, if they cannot come to an agreement within six months after my death, then as my executor shall determine."

If you want to leave specific items of tangible personal property to specific people, you can, of course, do so. Just don't forget to name who gets the balance of any tangible personal property you haven't specifically described. For example, "I give and bequeath my sterling silver tea service to Jane and the balance of all my other tangible personal property to my spouse, John." If you decide to give specific items to specific people, make sure you describe the item sufficiently so that there can be no doubt about which item you mean. "My engagement ring" may cause confusion whereas "my 1.75 carat square-cut diamond solitaire engagement ring set in platinum" may be a better description.

Make sure your attorney knows about any tangible personal property that is particularly valuable, such as valuable art or jewelry, or a valuable collection. In the interest of clarity, you may want to refer to such property specifically instead of having it pass under the general tangible personal property clause. For example, "I give and bequeath all of my tangible personal property, including my collection of twelve Monet watercolors, to Sally."

If your Will is unclear about whether or not an item is "tangible personal property," then state law will decide. For example, although money in a bank account typically is not tangible personal property, cash in the house or in a safe deposit box may be considered to be tangible personal property. If you're not sure whether an asset is tangible personal property, ask your attorney for clarification.

Example

Sam's Will specifies that all of his tangible personal property passes to Nancy, but that the residue of his estate passes to Claudia. After Sam's death, $10,000 in cash is discovered in the wall safe in his house. Does this $10,000 pass to Nancy, as part of the tangible personal property? Or does it pass to Claudia, as part of the residue?

It depends. If Sam's Will specifically states something like "I give my tangible personal property, including any household furniture and furnishings, automobiles, books, pictures, jewelry, art, clothing and other articles of household or personal use, but excluding coins held for investment and paper currency, to Nancy," then the cash passes to Claudia.

If the Will is not that specific, then it depends upon how "tangible personal property" is defined under the law of Sam's state.

Depending on the state where you live, you may be able to write a note or memorandum, separate from your Will, that lists specific items of tangible personal property and the person you want to receive each item. Then, if you change your mind, you can just change your list without having to change your Will. But be aware that in some states this type of note or memorandum is legally binding, while in others it is just a request that cannot be enforced legally. Make sure you know what the law is in your state.

Your Residuary Estate

The **residue** of your estate (also known as your **residuary estate**) is what remains after the payment of debts, expenses and taxes, the distribution of the tangible personal property, and the payment of any specific amounts you leave to anyone. Your Will must have a provision which disposes of the residue. For example, "I give, devise, and bequeath all the rest, residue and remainder of my property, both real and personal, of whatever kind and nature and wherever situated, to my spouse, John." This type of catch-all provision is known as the **residuary clause**.

You should name alternate beneficiaries of the residue in case your primary beneficiary dies before you do. For example, "I give, devise, and bequeath all the rest, residue and remainder of my property, both real and personal, of whatever kind and nature and wherever situated, to my spouse, John, if he survives me or, if he does not survive me, to my sister, Cathy, if she survives me or, if she does not survive me, to [name of a charity]."

What Does an Executor Do?

Your Will should also name an executor (and at least one alternate if the first executor is unable or unwilling to serve). Your executor is legally responsible for settling your estate. If you don't name an executor, or if all your named executors are unable or unwilling to serve, then the court will appoint an executor, but it may not be who you would have wanted.

Generally speaking, an executor:

- files the Will for probate if necessary,
- makes a diligent search for any assets of the deceased person; this may involve doing some detective work such as contacting financial institutions,

- safeguards the assets while the estate is being settled; for example, maintains any real estate, insures the property, and so on,
- pays all legitimate debts, expenses and taxes; this may involve determining whether or not a debt is legitimate, and
- distributes the remaining assets in accordance with the Will.

An executor's role is usually fairly short. Once the estate is fully settled (typically in a year or two), the executor's job is done.

Who Should You Choose as Your Executor?

You have a lot of choice in naming your executor. It can be any adult individual, such as a family member, friend, your accountant or your attorney. It can also be a corporate executor, such as a bank or trust company. If you wish, you can have more than one executor, who will act together as co-executors.

The most important consideration in choosing an executor is whether you trust that person to carry out your wishes, as expressed in your Will, as accurately, fairly and efficiently as possible. If you name co-executors, it is extremely important that they work well together. If not, you might be better served by naming a sole executor. You may feel that you should name all of your children as co-executors to avoid hurting anyone's feelings, and in some cases that may work out okay. But remember that this is not an honorary position; your executor has real legal rights and obligations. Be very cautious before you "include" a child as a co-executor who may cause problems for your estate, for example, someone who might fail to provide necessary information, might not meet court or other deadlines, or might be unhelpful to or disagreeable with the other co-executor(s).

In this day and age it is not particularly important to name an executor who lives close to you; most tasks can easily be done remotely. Also, as a practical matter, in most cases your executor will hire an attorney in the state where you live to help settle your estate.

Naming a Guardian for Your Child

If you have a minor child-that is, a child under the age of 18 or 21, depending on state law-then it is important that you name the person you would like the court to appoint as your child's legal guardian in the event a guardian is needed upon your death. Generally speaking, the court-appointed legal **guardian** (sometimes called a **conservator**) will have the rights and responsibilities of a parent, such as deciding where the child will live, what school he or she will attend, and the like.

Generally it is the court who ultimately decides who to appoint as guardian, based on the best interests of the child. The court doesn't necessarily have to appoint the person you name; however, your choice will be a strong factor in the court's decision. If you wish, you can name co-guardians. You should also name at least one alternate guardian in case your named guardian is unable or unwilling to accept the job.

Providing Financially for a Child

Although it is the court who appoints the guardian, you can decide who controls any money or other property that you leave for the benefit of a child.

In many states, a young child cannot directly inherit property of a value above a certain (small) amount. If you leave more than that amount to a child, the court will appoint someone to manage and control the property while the child is a minor. This court-appointed person is sometimes called a **custodian** or **conservator of the estate** of the child. When the child reaches the age of majority, the child automatically receives the property outright.

A much better way to provide financially for a child is to set up a trust for him or her. There are at least two major advantages to this: First, you get to appoint the person (the "trustee") who will manage the child's property, rather than leaving this important decision in the hands of a judge. Second, the child does not have to receive the property outright as soon as he or she reaches the age of majority. Instead, the trust can continue for as long as you like–even for the child's whole life. You can create the trust as part of your Will (see **Chapter 5, *Do You Need a Trust?***) or as part of a revocable living trust (see **Chapter 6, *Revocable Living Trusts***).

I am often asked whether it's better to name the same person as both guardian and trustee, or whether it's better to have different people in each of these roles. As with most things, there are pros and cons. On one hand, it may be easier for the guardian to access money for the support of the child without having to go through another person (the trustee). On the other hand, naming a separate guardian and trustee provides a system of checks and balances.

Other Will Provisions

The discussion above is by no means an exhaustive list of all of the provisions that can and should appear in a Will. There are many others. The important point is that, whatever provisions there are, your Will should be clear and unambiguous. You don't want controversies to arise after your death because your Will is subject to different interpretations.

Where Should You Keep Your Will?

State law and custom influence where you should keep your original, signed Will. In general, you should keep it in a safe place, because the original is needed for probate and to have your executor appointed. In some states, if your original Will cannot be found, then the law presumes that you intended to revoke it. Regardless of where you keep the original of your Will, you can, of course, keep copies at home for reference.

You may be inclined to keep the original in your safe deposit box. Whether you should do so depends on whether or not the person you named as your executor will be able to get into the box to retrieve the original of your Will.

In some states it may be just fine to keep your original Will in your safe deposit box because, after you die, your named executor will have easy access to your safe deposit box by, for example, simply showing the bank a copy of the Will in which he or she is named as the executor.

However, depending on your state's laws, your solely-owned safe deposit box may be sealed upon your death, in which case your named executor will need a court order to retrieve your original Will. In that case, you may be better off not keeping it in your safe deposit box. Some estate planning attorneys will offer to keep your original Will for you in their vault at no charge. Other options would be a safe or a fireproof file cabinet at home.

As with everything else, look to your attorney for guidance on the particular laws and customs in your state. Whichever way you go, make sure you are clear about where your original Will is located. It's also a good idea to tell your executor where to locate your Will. But you don't necessarily have to tell your executor what your Will says or give him or her a copy-that's entirely up to you.

You Need a Will Even if You Think You Don't

As we saw in **Chapter 2**, *The Number One Misconception About Wills*, many types of property don't pass by Will; namely, property that passes by beneficiary designation and property that passes by law. Moreover, as we will see in **Chapter 6**, *Revocable Living Trusts*, you can transform almost any property that would otherwise pass by Will into property that does not pass by Will by using a revocable living trust.

So you might not have any property that passes by Will. Then why bother having one?

In short, you need a Will as a default measure to handle any unexpected probate assets. In the course of settling your estate, your executor may find probate assets that were previously unknown, or may have been forgotten, or the like. For example, you may have thought that you and your spouse owned your cars as joint tenants with right of survivorship (no probate needed), when you really owned them as tenants in common (probate needed). Another common example would be if, after you die, your executor receives a refund check which is made out to you. In each of those cases, without a Will your share of the cars and the refund check, respectively, would pass by intestacy, which almost certainly isn't what you want.

Examples

Mr. & Mrs. Jones own their home as joint tenants with right of survivorship. They also own some joint bank accounts, their respective 401(k) accounts, and life insurance. They have named each other as the beneficiaries of the 401(k)s and the life insurance. Assume Mr. Jones dies. The house will pass to Mrs. Jones by law, as will the joint bank accounts. Mr. Jones' 401(k) and the life insurance upon his life will both pass to Mrs. Jones by beneficiary designation. There are no assets which would pass under a Will, that is, no probate assets. Why, then, would Mr. Jones need a Will?

Assume that the state where the Jones live has a small estate procedure for probate estates worth less than $30,000, and that the state's intestacy law provides that if there is a spouse and children, the spouse and children split the estate 50/50. Assume also that the Jones have adult children.

- Mr. Jones died with some accrued but unpaid vacation pay. Mr. Jones' employer sends a check made out to Mr. Jones. Since Mr. Jones is dead, Mrs. Jones will not be able to cash or deposit the check (not even into a joint bank account). The amount of the check is less than $30,000. If Mr. Jones has a Will which names Mrs. Jones as beneficiary, then the proceeds of the check can be distributed to Mrs. Jones under the small estate proceeding. If Mr. Jones does not have a Will, however, Mrs. Jones will have to split the proceeds of the check 50/50 with the adult children under the intestacy laws.

- After Mr. Jones' death, a check arrives in the mail for a manufacturer's rebate that Mr. Jones applied for before his death. Same result as above.

- After Mr. Jones' death, Mrs. Jones checks her state's unclaimed property database and discovers that the state is holding funds from an old bank account that Mr. Jones had long since forgotten about. The account was in Mr. Jones' sole name. Same result as above.

- ## *Remember*

  At a minimum your Will should clearly and unambiguously:

  spell out who receives your tangible personal property and how it is to be divided (to avoid disagreements),

  name residuary beneficiaries and alternate residuary beneficiaries (to avoid intestacy),

  name your executor and alternate executor,

  name a guardian and an alternate guardian (if you have young children), and

  include a trust to hold assets you leave to any young children.

CHAPTER 4

What Happens if You Become Incapacitated?

Let's switch gears now and discuss how estate planning can help, not just upon death, but also if age, illness or injury leaves you incapacitated during your life. Each state has its legal definition of incapacity, but in general an **incapacitated** person is someone who is impaired to the point of being incapable of making or communicating responsible decisions concerning themselves or their property.

What Happens Without Prior Planning?

Without prior planning, if you become incapacitated, a legal **guardianship** proceeding may be required-that is, a court proceeding in which the judge:

- determines whether or not you are, indeed, legally incapacitated, and
- appoints a **guardian** (sometimes called a **conservator**) to handle your affairs, if necessary.

The judge can appoint a guardian to make all your personal decisions, such as where you will live (a guardian of the person), and/or a guardian to handle all your assets (a guardian of the estate). There may also be other types of proceedings that allow for lesser degrees of guardianship if you are not totally incapacitated.

In any event, a guardianship or similar proceeding is likely to be complicated, lengthy, expensive, and public. Your prospective guardian will likely need to hire an attorney, and the court will probably appoint another attorney to represent you, the incapacitated person, as well. A guardianship may also be contentious if more than one person wants to be the guardian or if the allegedly incapacitated person does not agree that he or she is incapacitated.

"Putting Someone's Name" on Your Accounts

You may be tempted to "put someone else's name" on your bank accounts for convenience. For example, you may have considered "putting your daughter's name" on your checking account so that if you become incapacitated, your daughter will be able to write checks. You might do this without giving it much thought. Unfortunately, that may lead to unintended and unwelcome consequences because, legally, it typically makes your daughter a **joint owner** of the account.

From the bank's perspective, adding a joint owner sounds like a good idea. It's much easier for a bank or other financial institution to deal with a joint owner than with an agent under a power of attorney (discussed below). Although powers of attorney generally have the force of law, and in many states financial institutions are required by law to accept validly executed powers of attorney, the bank may be wary of a power of attorney because it might not be valid, or may have been revoked without the bank's knowledge.

From an estate planning perspective, however, making someone a joint owner could have extremely undesirable consequences for you in two ways. First, a joint owner of your bank account typically has the right to inherit all of the money in the account upon your death *regardless of what your Will says*. This consequence was illustrated in Quiz #1 in **Chapter 2, *The Number One Misconception About Wills.***

In addition, "putting someone's name" on your account may give that person important legal rights to the money in the account during your life. Because the person is now an owner of the account, there is always the possibility that the person could withdraw money from the account without your knowledge, or that the account could be taken by the person's creditors.

Therefore, it's usually best to use a power of attorney to name an agent to manage your accounts. We'll discuss how to do this in the next section, ***Using a Power of Attorney for Finances.*** Be sure to see the Examples at the end of that section.

You can also use a revocable living trust, together with a power of attorney, to help manage your finances if you become incapacitated. See ***Using a Revocable Living Trust in Case of Incapacity*** in **Chapter 6.**

Using a Power of Attorney for Finances

In order to avoid the expense, delay and other problems associated with guardianship, you will typically sign a **power of attorney** as part of the estate planning process. The power of attorney is a legal document in which you (called the **principal**) appoint one or more people to be your **agent** (sometimes called your **attorney-in-fact**). The purpose of signing a power of attorney is so that your agent has the legal authority to take certain actions for you without having to be your court-appointed guardian.

What Your Agent Can and Can't Do

Your agent is empowered only to take actions for your benefit. Your agent must not use the power of attorney for his or her own benefit. For example, in dealing with your car, your agent typically could *not* legally:

- sell it and keep the proceeds for himself,
- give it to his daughter (or allow his daughter to drive it-no matter how badly she needs a car),
- sell it to someone for a price below market value,
- give it to charity, or
- junk it without receiving market value for it.

Your agent could, however, sell your car (at market value) if the proceeds were needed to provide for you. The same goes for *any of your other property.*

Also, although the agent may be called an attorney-in-fact, this does not mean that the agent is an attorney or has the powers of an attorney!

The power of attorney document specifies the powers you give to your agent. The type of power of attorney you would typically sign as part of your estate planning is commonly known as a **general power of attorney** or a **general durable power of attorney**. This means you give your agent broad and sweeping powers-basically the power to take any actions with respect to your property that you yourself could take (limited, of course, by the agent's duty to take actions only for your benefit). For example, the power to enter into business transactions, financial and banking transactions, real estate transactions, deal with tax matters, social security matters, pension plans and retirement accounts, and the like. That way, if you become incapacitated, your agent has the legal authority to take any action needed for your benefit, without the necessity of being appointed your legal guardian. If the powers are not broad enough, you run the risk that your agent will have to go to court to get additional authority.

There have been many cases of agents abusing their authority under a power of attorney. That's why it's vitally important that you have a high level of trust in the person you name as your agent, and that your prospective agent understands what he or she can and cannot do as your agent.

Your power of attorney should also be clear as to whether or not your agent has the authority to pay himself or herself a fee for acting as your agent. You may or may not wish to compensate a family member for the time he or she devotes to acting as your agent. That is entirely up to you. If your agent is a professional (attorney, accountant, financial advisor and the like) typically he or she will be compensated for acting as your agent.

If someone (for example, another family member) thinks that your agent is abusing his or her authority, that person can alert the court, in which case the court may require your agent to **account** for his or her actions. If this happens, your agent would have to submit paperwork to the court (an **accounting**) that shows in detail what actions your agent has taken by authority of the power of attorney.

When the Power Begins

It is important to understand when the agent's authority begins. You may think that your agent cannot act until you become incapacitated. But that is not the case. Typically, your general power of attorney is effective as soon as you sign it and give it to your agent. Once that happens, your agent can act whether you are incapacitated or not.

So, hypothetically speaking, if you execute a general power of attorney and give it to your agent today, your agent can theoretically go to your bank and wipe out your bank accounts immediately. Of course the agent is not legally permitted to steal from you, but a general power of attorney permits your agent to withdraw the money even though you are not incapacitated. You should trust your agent enough to be comfortable that he or she will not act under the power of attorney unless you become incapacitated (or you specifically ask him or her to act on your behalf-for example, if you're traveling out of the country and need something to be signed).

If you're not comfortable with the idea of your agent being able to act when you aren't incapacitated, you may want to use a different type of power of attorney called a **springing power of attorney**. A springing power of attorney still gives your agent broad and sweeping powers to do anything you could do yourself, but the difference is that it does not "spring" into effect until a specified condition happens, typically that you become incapacitated, as certified by your doctor.

Each type of power of attorney has its pros and cons. A general power of attorney is much simpler for your agent to use, but requires a certain level of trust. A springing power of attorney is much more complicated to use. It may be difficult or impossible for your agent to get a physician's certification (or whatever else is required by the condition) due to privacy laws (such as HIPAA). Third parties may also be less likely to accept a springing power of attorney because of concerns that the requirements have not been met. Which one you should use depends on your specific situation and personal comfort level.

When the Power Ends

You can change or revoke a power of attorney at any time, as long as you have the mental capacity to do so. As a legal matter this is usually done by signing a new power of attorney which states that you revoke all prior powers of attorney, or by signing a revocation of the power of attorney. As a practical matter, you should destroy all originals of the old power of attorney so that no one can attempt to use them. For this reason, it's sometimes a good idea to keep the originals in your possession, rather than giving them to your agent (but let your agent know where to find them should the need arise).

A power of attorney is no longer effective after you die. At that point, it is your executor who will take over handling your property. Agents sometimes think that they can continue to write checks or otherwise deal with property after the death of the principal, but in general they have no legal authority to do this.

If the Power Is Refused

What if the bank or other financial institution refuses to accept your agent's power of attorney? A bank could also claim that the bank's own form of power of attorney is the only one it will accept. Regardless of a bank's policies, powers of attorney generally have the force of law, and in many states financial institutions are required by law to accept validly executed powers of attorney.

If you're concerned that your financial institution will refuse to accept your power of attorney when the time comes, then you should have the financial institution establish in its records, in advance, that your agent is the attorney-in-fact on the account. Check with your financial institution to find out how to do this.

Examples

Jane, a widow, is concerned about who will do her banking, pay her bills, and so on if she becomes incapacitated. She would like her daughter, Debby, to be able to handle these matters for her without Debby having to go to court and be appointed as guardian. Jane goes to her bank and "puts Debby's name" on her accounts. The bank has Debby sign a signature card so that she is the joint owner of the accounts with her mother. Years pass and then:

- Debby is involved in a messy divorce. When she has to disclose her assets, her husband's lawyer points out that she is the owner of joint bank accounts. The bank accounts may become part of the marital assets to be divided up between Debby and her husband.

- Debby develops a drug, drinking, or gambling problem. She becomes desperate for cash and realizes that she is the joint owner of bank accounts – Hurrah! She goes into the bank and withdraws the money.

- Debby is in a car accident. There is a lawsuit and a judgment against her for more than her insurance will cover. All her assets, including the joint bank accounts, are subject to this judgment.

Jane's better choice would have been to execute a power of attorney naming her daughter as agent and presenting it to the bank to establish Debby as the agent (not the joint owner) on the accounts.

A power of attorney not only avoids the unpleasantness of the three scenarios above, but it could also allow Debby, as agent, to deal with many other matters for her mother, such as handling other assets, filing tax returns, and more.

Note that the same types of problems can also arise if you "put your house in someone else's name," which from a legal point of view may be akin to giving your house away. It may also create tax problems that are beyond the scope of this book. Before you do anything like that, consult your estate planning attorney.

Making Your Healthcare Wishes Known

It is a good idea to include advance directives as part of the estate planning process. **Advance directives** are legally binding documents that deal with health care matters. They are known by many different names in different states, but they typically address the following:

- Your wishes regarding life support systems, such as artificially administered nutrition and hydration, mechanical respiration, and cardiopulmonary resuscitation (CPR), if you are terminally ill or permanently unconscious, and not capable of communicating your wishes. Depending on your state, you might address these matters in a stand-alone document called a **Living Will** or as part of a **Health Care Power of Attorney** or other advance directive document.

- The appointment of an agent to make health care decisions for you if you are not capable of making them yourself. You might do this in a Health Care Power of Attorney or as part of another type of advance directive document.

- Your wishes regarding organ donation. In many states, you can use your Living Will, Health Care Power of Attorney or other advance directive document to specify whether or not you wish to donate organs and, if you do, which organs. Or you may specify that you want your agent to make the decision.

Be sure that you understand the specific language and consequences of the documents used in your state. In addition to your attorney, you may also want to consult your physician if you have any questions about specific medical treatments or how your health care documents will work in specific situations.

- ## *Remember*

  Generally speaking:

  If you sign a general power of attorney, it can be used by the person you name (your agent) even if you are not incapacitated.

  Your agent under a power of attorney is authorized to act only in your best interest.

  Your agent's power under a power of attorney ends upon your death.

  "Putting someone's name" on your bank account can not only give that person important legal rights to the money in the account during your life, but can also give that person the right to inherit all the money in the account upon your death, regardless of what your Will says.

CHAPTER 5

Do You Need
a Trust?

Trusts are important and useful tools in estate planning, but that doesn't mean they're for everyone. You can't know whether or not you need a trust without knowing what you're trying to accomplish by having a trust and whether the type of trust you're considering will do the job. In this chapter I'll introduce some basic types of trusts, along with their common uses.

What Exactly Is a Trust?

Broadly speaking, a **trust** is an arrangement by which a person or institution, the **trustee**, legally owns the property of one person, the **grantor**, for the benefit of another person, the **beneficiary**. Here is a common, and simple, example:

> Mrs. B., who has a six-year-old son, Timmy, is making
> out her Will. Because it is undesirable to leave a large

amount of money to a minor child, the Will includes a trust for Timmy. The Will may say something like, "I give and bequeath to my Trustee, John Doe, the sum of X dollars, to be held, administered and disposed of as follows. My Trustee is authorized to pay from time to time so much, or none, of the net income of the trust as may be advisable, in the discretion of my Trustee, for the health, education, maintenance and support of my son, Timmy. When my said son reaches the age of 25 years, my Trustee shall distribute to my said son the entire balance of the trust."

There are generally three parties to a trust:

- The grantor (sometimes also known as the settlor, the trustor or by other names) is the person who intends to place property in trust. In the above example, Mrs. B is the grantor.
- The trustee is the person or institution who legally owns the property for the benefit of another person, and is charged with safeguarding, investing and distributing the property as directed by the terms of the trust. In the above example, John Doe is the trustee.
- The beneficiary is the person who will receive the benefit of the property, but only under the terms of the trust. In the above example, Timmy is the beneficiary.

A trust divides property ownership into two separate pieces – **legal ownership** and **beneficial ownership**. The trustee is the legal owner of the property in the trust, and the beneficiary is the beneficial owner of the property in the trust.

In our example above, John Doe, as trustee, is the legal owner of the property in the trust. However, he cannot use the property for his own benefit because he is not the beneficial owner. He can use the property only for the legitimate expenses of the trust and for the benefit of Timmy, who is the beneficial owner of the property in the trust.

John Doe will be legally obligated to safeguard and invest the trust property until Timmy is 25 years old. During that time, John Doe will also decide when and how much of the trust money to spend for Timmy's health, education, maintenance and support. When Timmy turns 25 years old, John Doe will pay to Timmy whatever property remains in the trust and the trust will terminate.

Why You May Want a Trust

Trusts can be extremely useful in estate planning, and there are many different types of trusts that are used for many different purposes. Here is a sample of some of the reasons you may want a trust as part of your estate plan:

- If you are leaving assets to a minor child. As we have seen, a trustee can manage the assets until the child reaches a certain age.
- If you are leaving assets to a beneficiary who may not be capable of managing money, or who may not want to manage money, such as an elderly or inexperienced person. A trustee can manage and distribute the assets for the benefit of that person.
- If you leave assets to someone who is disabled and receives government benefits (or may be entitled to receive government benefits in the future), you may

inadvertently disqualify that person from receiving benefits. You can avoid that outcome by using a certain type of legally sanctioned trust (usually called a "special needs trust" or "supplemental needs trust").

- If you leave assets to a beneficiary who may have unpaid creditors, such as a beneficiary with problems managing money, drug or alcohol problems, marital problems, or who is in a profession with a high risk of being sued, you can use a trust to protect assets from the beneficiary's creditors.

- If you are in a second marriage and have children from a prior marriage. In this situation, if you die first and leave assets to your spouse, there is no guarantee that your spouse will leave anything to your children when he or she later dies. Instead, you can create a certain type of trust, sometimes called a marital trust or a QTIP trust. With this type of trust, the trust property is used for the benefit of your surviving spouse as long as he or she lives, and then whatever is left goes to your children (or whoever else you specify).

- If your estate may be subject to estate taxes. There are certain types of trusts used for estate tax minimization.

- If you want to avoid probate. In **What Is Probate?** in **Chapter 1**, we discussed some of the factors you might want to consider in deciding whether the benefits of avoiding probate are worth the costs. One way to avoid probate is by using a revocable living trust, which we will discuss in more detail in the next chapter.

- If you are concerned that you may become incapacitated. In the last chapter, we discussed using a power of attorney in case you are incapacitated. A revocable living trust is another tool that can be useful if you are incapacitated, and we will discuss that in more detail in the next chapter.

Two Types of Trusts

Your trust can be one of two distinct types. Let's look at the characteristics and consequences of each.

Testamentary trusts. One type is a trust you create by including trust language in your Will (as Mrs. B. did in our example). This is known as a "trust under Will" or **testamentary trust**. Some of the characteristics of a testamentary trust are as follows:

- A testamentary trust legally exists only after you die and your Will is probated.
- Because the trust doesn't exist until after you die, you can't also be the trustee of your testamentary trust.
- Likewise, because the trust doesn't exist until after you die, you can't fund your testamentary trust during your life. A bit later, I'll explain what it means to "fund" your trust.

Living trusts. The other type is a trust you create by using a separate, stand-alone legal document. This is known as an "intervivos" or **living trust**. Some of the characteristics of a living trust are as follows:

- A living trust is created during your life. It legally exists when you sign the trust document with the necessary legal formalities.

- You can be both the grantor and the trustee of your living trust. The fact that the living trust exists during your lifetime makes this possible.
- You can fund your living trust during your life. That is, you can choose to transfer legal title to property to the trustee. The fact that the living trust exists during your lifetime makes this possible.

How a Trust Is Created

A trust is usually created in writing by a legal document (the **trust document**). As we just discussed, the legal document which creates the trust can be a Will, or instead it can be a type of contract between the grantor and the trustee. This type of contract is traditionally called a trust indenture or **trust agreement**, but it may also be called by other names.

The trust is **created** by a valid trust document, that is, a probated Will or a properly signed trust agreement. The trust document spells out:

- the terms and conditions the trustee must follow when dealing with property in the trust,
- when the trust will end, and
- how the remaining property will be distributed when the trust ends.

How a Trust Is Funded

It is important to distinguish the concept of creating a trust from the concept of funding a trust. Although you may have validly created a trust (by your Will or with a trust agreement), it is not **funded** until you transfer property to the trust. In other words, the trust is funded only when the trustee legally owns some property, known as the **trust property**. (Trust property is sometimes called the "trust corpus" or other names).

The way you fund a testamentary trust is by leaving property to your trustee in your Will. For example, "I give and bequeath my residuary estate to my trustee, in trust, to be held, administered and distributed as follows..." The way you fund a living trust is by transferring property to your trustee, either during your life (for example, by making your trustee the owner of your bank account) or by Will.

What Does a Trustee Do?

The trustee is the person you are "trusting" to safeguard and invest the trust property, pay all the legitimate debts, expenses and taxes of the trust, and distribute the remaining property in accordance with the terms of the trust document.

A trustee's role is similar to that of an executor, but with some important differences. While an executor's job is fairly short, typically lasting a year or two until the estate is settled, the role of a trustee can continue for many years.

Another important difference is that, unlike an executor who usually has little flexibility, a trustee may be called upon to exercise **discretion**. This means that if the trust tells the trustee to use the trust property for the "health, maintenance and support" of a beneficiary, it will be up to the trustee to decide specifically what may be desirable for the beneficiary's "health, maintenance and support."

These decisions may be extremely difficult for any number of reasons. For example, let's say the trust was established because the beneficiary is a spendthrift. The beneficiary might demand that the trustee pay for a new sports car or pay off the beneficiary's credit card bills. The trustee will need to decide if such expenditures are a prudent use of the trust funds. The trustee may have to consider many factors, such as the size of the trust fund and the beneficiary's other income.

As another example, let's say there is more than one beneficiary of the trust. Should the trustee expend more money on one beneficiary than another? What if one of the beneficiaries needs medical care that, if paid for by the trust, would leave very little for the other beneficiaries? Should the trustee pay for that?

Sometimes these types of questions are answered by the express terms of the trust, but many times they are not. The trustee, therefore, is the one who will need to decide.

Who Should You Name as Your Trustee?

As with naming an executor, you have a lot of choice in choosing a trustee. Your trustee can be any adult individual, such as a family member, friend, your accountant, or your attorney. Another possibility is a corporate trustee, such as a bank or trust company.

Your trust may have more than one trustee, who must act together as co-trustees. If you have more than two trustees, usually the majority rules. As with co-executors, it's very important that your co-trustees work well together. For example, although it may be tempting to "include" all of your children as co-trustees, if they cannot agree, they may have to get the court involved to resolve disputes.

One advantage to having a corporate trustee, such as a bank or trust company, is that they are professionals who are used to dealing with issues of discretion. Typically, a corporate trustee will have an experienced committee to deal with requests from beneficiaries. Bear in mind that the trust may have to be a certain minimum value in order for a bank or trust company to agree to act as trustee.

Another option that works well in some situations is to have two co-trustees, one of whom is an individual familiar with the beneficiaries and the family situation, and the other of whom is a professional corporate trustee.

If you are considering a corporate trustee, you may want to meet with a few banks or trust companies in advance in order to get a sense of how they work, what they charge for their services, and whether they would meet your needs. Your attorney may be able to refer you to some reputable corporate trustees. If you choose a corporate trustee, make sure the trust provides a method for replacing the corporate trustee with a different corporate trustee in case situations change, such as a corporate merger or changes in personnel.

- ## *Remember*

  Do you need a trust? Check some of the reasons you might want one, which are listed in this chapter.

  Before you set up a trust, know why you're doing it.

  There is more than one way to create a trust. You can create a trust either by including trust language in your Will (a "testamentary trust") or by a separate document (a "living trust").

CHAPTER 6

Revocable
Living Trusts

You may have heard the term **revocable living trust** (which I'll refer to as an "RLT"). RLTs have become important, useful, and much talked about tools in estate planning, but what are they exactly? More important, do you "need" one? As with other estate planning tools, you should know first what you want to accomplish, and second whether an RLT is the best way to meet your goals.

What Is a Revocable Living Trust?

An RLT is a stand-alone legal document that creates one or more trusts. In other words, you don't set it up in your Will, but in a separate document that works in conjunction with your Will. It's called a "living" trust because it exists while you're alive. It's a "revocable" trust because you can change or revoke its terms, or even revoke the whole thing, if your situation changes.

An RLT is also sometimes called a "Will substitute." That's because, just like a Will, an RLT can specify who gets the trust property when you die. Property you own in an RLT passes according to the terms of the RLT, *regardless of what your Will says.*

In its simplest form, an RLT tells the trustee how to use the trust property during your life, as well as how the remaining trust property must be distributed upon your death.

An RLT can also contain within it other types of trusts, for example, a trust for a minor child as in the example in **Chapter 5, *Do You Need a Trust?*.** You can think of an RLT as a container for different types of trusts, much as you can think of an IRA as a container for different types of investments.

Do You Need a Revocable Living Trust?

As we saw in **Chapter 1, *Basics You'll Want to Know*,** an RLT is an optional part of an estate plan and works together with your Will, power of attorney and advance directives to create your total estate plan. It will cost you additional time and money not only to set up the RLT, but also to fund it with your assets.

Many times when I ask clients why they "need" an RLT, they have no idea. Some just hem and haw, some just give a vague (or incorrect) answer, but eventually what it comes down to is that they don't know. I have found this to be the case both with clients who don't yet have an RLT and with clients who have already spent considerable time and money to set up an RLT.

In the rest of this chapter, we'll discuss two of the major and most important uses of RLTs:

- using an RLT to avoid probate, and
- using an RLT to help if you become incapacitated.

Your attorney might suggest other reasons why an RLT would be useful in your situation.

The next section will help you consider whether you want to avoid probate. Let's say you do want to avoid probate. Does that mean you "need" an RLT? Not necessarily. Re-read **Chapter 2,** *The Number One Misconception About Wills,* and remember that property that passes by beneficiary designation (such as life insurance, IRAs, 401(k)s, annuities, pensions and the like) already avoids probate. So does property that passes by law (such as jointly-owned property).

If your goal is to avoid probate, then an RLT is one option you can use (along with others). If you use an RLT, you should still have a Will (see *You Still Need a Pourover Will* later in this chapter).

Why Avoid Probate?

In **Chapter 1,** *Basics You'll Want to Know,* we talked about probate, which is a legal proceeding in which a deceased person's Will is submitted to a court. The court then determines whether or not the Will is valid and appoints an executor to carry out the terms of the Will. There is usually ongoing court supervision of the progress of the estate administration and certain requirements the executor will have to fulfill before the estate can legally be closed.

We also talked about the popular misconception that probate must be avoided at all costs. But the reality is that it depends. Probate procedures vary enormously, not only from state to state, but even from court to court. Let's discuss in more detail some of the factors that might make you want to avoid probate where you live. Your attorney can guide you based on his or her experience with probate in your jurisdiction.

Probate May Be Slow and Burdensome

In some places the probate process is simple and quick, while in others it is slow, expensive and burdensome. You may feel that the probate process in your state adds value; for example, by having a judge oversee the settlement of your estate; or you may feel that the process is more bureaucratic in nature and something you would rather avoid.

Probate May Be Expensive

Probate fees vary enormously from state to state; they usually depend on the value of property. In some states you can avoid probate fees by placing property in an RLT, but in others the probate fee is computed on the value of *all* property, not just probate property. If your state has high probate fees that you can avoid by placing property in an RLT, you might want to do that in order to take advantage of that opportunity.

Probate May Require Court Involvement in Trusts

Some states require ongoing court supervision of trusts created by Will (testamentary trusts), but not of living trusts, like an RLT. What does this mean?

Say you want to create a trust for a minor child, and that you want the trust to exist until the child is 25 years old. If the child is young, the trust may have to exist for many years.

In the case of this particular type of trust, you have the choice of two ways of creating the trust. You could create it as part of your Will (a testamentary trust), or you could create the trust as part of your RLT.

If you create the trust by Will (a testamentary trust), state law may require the trustee to submit annual accountings to the court for its approval. This requirement creates an additional expense for the trust and adds a burden of both time and energy on the part of the trustee. On the other hand, if you create the trust in an RLT, normally the trustee is not required to obtain judicial approval of annual accounts (unless the trustee or a beneficiary specifically requests it). If this is the case in your state, you may want an RLT to avoid the expense and delay of ongoing court supervision of your trusts.

Of course, if you prefer to have the court monitor the actions of your trustee, then you might be better off with a testamentary trust. Your attorney can help you evaluate your options.

Probate May Be Delayed by Hard-to-Find Heirs

As we discussed in **What Happens to Your Property if You Don't Have a Will?** in **Chapter 3**, your legal heirs are those relatives who, under state law, would inherit your estate if you die without a Will. A legal heir who you don't name as a beneficiary in your Will would be better off if your Will were declared invalid. Therefore, the law generally requires that your legal heirs be given notice of a probate proceeding so that if a legal heir has any reason to think your Will is not valid, then he or she can raise an objection in court.

> Example
>
> John has three children, Tom, Dick and Harry. When John writes his Will, he leaves his entire estate to Tom and Dick, but does not leave anything to Harry. Although Tom, Dick and Harry are all John's legal heirs, only Tom and Dick are beneficiaries under John's Will. Therefore, it would be better for Harry if the Will were declared invalid so that he could inherit under the intestacy laws.

Some states simply require your heirs to be notified, by regular mail, once your Will has been probated and your executor has been appointed. But beware if you live in a state that requires your legal heirs to be notified before the court will probate your Will and appoint your executor. If you have hard-to-find legal heirs, the resulting delay can be a problem if there are assets that need to be dealt with, such as financial securities that need to be sold right away. The court may appoint a "temporary" administrator to deal with these issues, but that adds another layer of bureaucratic expense and delay.

By avoiding probate, you may be able to eliminate the legal heir notification requirements.

Probate May Encourage Will Contests

As we saw in the last section, some states simply require your legal heirs to be notified by regular mail once your executor has been appointed. If a troublesome heir wants to contest your Will, he or she has to take the initiative to do so.

But beware if you live in a state that requires that your legal heirs sign a paper consenting to the probate, or be served with a legal summons, before your Will can be probated. Besides the obvious expense, delay and potential difficulty of such a process, it may give a troublesome heir the mistaken impression that he or she somehow has a right to inherit under your Will. In other words, it may encourage a legal heir to contest your Will, which is not desirable from your point of view.

By avoiding probate, you may be able to eliminate the legal heir notification requirements. Your attorney can also help you evaluate other ways an RLT can prevent problems if you have troublesome heirs.

Probate May Compromise Your Privacy

Generally speaking, a Will becomes a public document after probate. If you were so inclined, you could walk into most probate courts, sit down, and read any of the Wills that had been probated there over the years.

If your Will is complicated-that is, if it includes many different types of assets and/or makes many bequests to specific individuals or charities, or if you have an unusual or potentially embarrassing family situation-a public document is probably not what you want.

For example, let's say you want to leave certain items of jewelry to specific individuals. In a Will, such items have to be described with specificity, so that there is no doubt as to which item is being bequeathed. The Will, therefore, might say something like, "I give and bequeath my two-carat emerald ring with 24 prong-set diamonds total weight 1.1 carats set in a white gold band to Jane." You might not want the world to know that Jane now owns such a valuable piece of jewelry.

Or let's say that you have three children. Your Will divides your estate equally among them, but one of your children is bad with money, has a drinking or drug problem, or has marital difficulties, or the like. That child's share is to be held in trust during the child's life. Is that something you want in a public document?

Finally, let's just say that your Will is very long and complicated and goes on for pages and pages. That may be a case of "too much information" to reveal in a public document.

In addition, as part of the probate process, your executor is usually required to file a list of all the assets you owned at your death (an inventory) and an accounting that shows exactly what property and how much property each of your beneficiaries received from your estate. In some states these are also public documents. That is an even more frightening proposition than having the Will be public, and may be something you want to avoid.

What's the alternative? You could instead esta
RLT which has the same provisions as a Will. The di
is that, generally speaking, an RLT remains a
document, not a public one. Depending on your state s laws,
merely creating the RLT may be enough to keep your wishes
private. Or you may also need to fund the RLT and avoid
probate altogether in order to maintain privacy. Your lawyer
can give you more specific information about how the
process works in your state.

Using a Revocable Living Trust to Avoid Probate

How exactly does an RLT avoid probate? When you die,
property owned in your RLT is transferred according to the
terms of your RLT (no probate needed), not according to
your Will (probate needed). Therefore, an RLT can be used
to turn probate property into non-probate property!

In order for this to happen, you can't simply *create* the
RLT by a signed trust document. You have to go a step
further and *fund* your RLT during your life. That means that
you have to transfer ownership of the property to the trustee.

For example, let's say you have a bank account in your
sole name. Since that type of an asset passes by Will, then
when you die, there will have to be a probate proceeding (or
at least a small estate proceeding) in order to have the bank
account transferred to the person you name in your Will.

If instead you create an RLT (step 1), and then transfer
ownership of your bank account to the trustee (step 2), then
when you die, the bank account will be distributed according

to the terms of your RLT. It does not pass by Will and voilà, no probate!

You transfer different types of assets to an RLT in different ways. For example, you typically transfer real estate by signing a new deed; you typically transfer a financial account by changing the ownership of the account with the financial institution; you typically transfer a car at the DMV, and so on. In order to avoid probate, you need to be as thorough as possible in executing this step.

It can be quite an investment of time, energy, and money to transfer assets to an RLT, and that's why I want you to be sure that avoiding probate is worth it, and that you have considered other options. Make sure you know what steps are involved for each of your assets. Many people get bogged down with this step and don't follow through.

Do You Lose Control of Your Assets?

But if you transfer ownership of your assets to a trustee, doesn't that mean you lose control of them during your lifetime?! No – typically you will be both the grantor and the trustee during your life. In addition, your RLT will typically provide that you can withdraw property from the trust at any time. Finally, your RLT is revocable, so that you can amend or revoke the whole thing at any time. Because it is revocable, it has no effect on your taxes and cannot be used to protect assets from your creditors.

So, generally speaking, if you transfer assets to your RLT, you will still be able to deal with those assets in every respect the way you could before. As a practical matter, the only difference will be in the name of the legal owner.

Example

John Doe creates an RLT. The document that creates the RLT says that during John Doe's lifetime, he is both the grantor and the trustee of the RLT. John Doe has a bank account. When John Doe gets his bank statement, it shows that the owner of the account is "John Doe." John Doe contacts his bank and has them transfer the ownership of the account to his RLT. The bank records will then show that the owner is "John Doe, as Trustee of the John Doe Revocable Living Trust dated _____." John Doe, as trustee, can continue to deal with the account in the same way he did before he transferred it into the RLT.

When John Doe dies, any money in the account will be transferred as specified in the RLT, regardless of what John Doe's Will says (and so without probate).

You Still Need a Pourover Will

Even if you have an RLT, you still need to have a Will. Typically an RLT will be prepared along with a type of Will called a **pourover Will**. A pourover Will simply says that your entire probate estate should be paid over to the trustee of your RLT and distributed in accordance with the terms of your RLT.

For example, a pourover Will might say something like "I give, devise and bequeath all of my property, both real and personal, to the Trustee under a certain Revocable Living Trust dated _____, to hold, manage and control such property under the terms of said trust, and to distribute the proceeds to the beneficiaries therein named according to the terms and conditions of said Revocable Living Trust at the time of my death."

If you are planning to fund your RLT with all of your assets so that at your death you have no probate assets, then why do you need a pourover Will? In short, you still need a pourover Will as a default measure to handle any unexpected probate assets or assets that must be probate assets (see *You Need a Will Even if You Think You Don't*, and the examples in **Chapter 3**).

Using a Revocable Living Trust in Case of Incapacity

Besides avoiding probate, you can also use an RLT in case you become incapacitated.

In *Using a Power of Attorney for Finances* in **Chapter 4**, we discussed using a power of attorney to give someone you appoint (your agent) the power to deal with your financial assets. You need a power of attorney to avoid a legal guardianship or other court proceeding if you become incapacitated.

An RLT is another way to plan for incapacity. Your RLT would state you are the trustee during your lifetime, but if you become incapacitated, the role of trustee is taken over by a successor trustee (who you name). If the RLT is funded, then the successor trustee can take over managing the assets in the RLT *without a power of attorney*.

An RLT also lets you define the circumstances under which you will be considered incapacitated. For example, it could say something like "The Grantor shall be considered incapacitated only if so declared by a court of competent jurisdiction or if by reason of illness or mental or physical disability is, in the opinion of two licensed physicians, unable properly to handle the Grantor's own affairs." Or it could say simply that you will be considered incapacitated just because the successor trustee declares it to be so – the determination does not necessarily have to involve physicians. Essentially you can provide any definition of incapacity you want, tailored to your specific comfort level.

Remember that in order to use your RLT successfully in planning for incapacity, it must be funded. In other words, upon your incapacity, the successor trustee will only have control over assets that you have transferred to the RLT.

In *"Putting Someone's Name" on Your Accounts* in **Chapter 4**, we saw that a financial institution may be wary of a power of attorney which it thinks may not be valid, or may have been revoked without its knowledge. Financial institutions may be more willing to deal with a successor trustee than with an agent under a power of attorney. Of course, the financial institution may require that the successor trustee sign an affidavit to the effect that the conditions specified in the RLT have been met, and may have other requirements before permitting the successor trustee to take over as trustee.

Be aware that even if you use an RLT to plan for incapacity, you should still have a power of attorney as a default measure to handle any unexpected assets outside of the RLT. For example, there may be an asset you forgot to transfer to the RLT. It is also extremely important to have a power of attorney to handle assets which cannot be held within the RLT. Important examples of this are your IRAs and 401(k)s, which cannot be owned by your RLT.

Example

Let's take the example of Jane and her daughter, Debby, which we discussed in *"Putting Someone's Name" on Your Accounts* in **Chapter 4**. Jane was a widow who wanted her daughter, Debby, to be able to handle banking and bill paying chores for her without having to go to court to be appointed as guardian. We discussed two of the options available to Jane, either making Debby the joint owner of the account, or making Debby her agent under a power of attorney.

Another option would be for Jane to set up an RLT. The RLT document would name Jane as the initial trustee and Debby as the successor trustee. The successor trustee would take over as trustee in the event of Jane's death or incapacity. Jane would then transfer ownership of her bank accounts from herself, as an individual, to herself as trustee of the RLT. The bank accounts would then be part of the assets of the RLT. If Jane became incapacitated, then Debby, as successor trustee, would be able to control and manage the assets for Jane.

However, Jane should still execute a power of attorney naming Debby as agent. Why?

- After Jane becomes incapacitated, assets may be discovered which are not owned in the RLT, for example, a refund check made out to Jane in her sole name.

- After Jane becomes incapacitated, Debby realizes that she is going to need to withdraw funds from her mother's IRA or 401(k) in order to pay for her mother's medical expenses. Debby will need a power of attorney in order to do this.

- ## *Remember*

  You might want a revocable living trust if you want to avoid probate or if you become incapacitated in the future.

  You could save significant expense by avoiding probate, depending on where you live. Check the reasons to avoid probate in this chapter against the procedures in your probate court.

  Having a revocable living trust allows you to name someone to take over managing your assets if you become incapacitated.

  If you are using a revocable living trust to avoid probate or to plan for future incapacity, you should not only <u>create</u> the trust, but also <u>fund</u> it with your assets.

CHAPTER 7

Working With an Attorney

One of the most important decisions you'll make in setting up your estate plan is your choice of an attorney. In this chapter I'll cover why you need an attorney and help you choose the right one.

Why You Need an Attorney

The job of an estate planning attorney is to help you plan your estate to minimize controversy and maximize benefits to your beneficiaries after your death. In other words, a good estate planning attorney will keep your estate and your beneficiaries *out* of court – both by minimizing probate court involvement and, even more importantly, by preventing Will contests and other expensive legal battles.

An estate plan that is ambiguous or confusing, that doesn't make sense, or that encourages beneficiaries to contest your

Will, may be in the best interests of the lawyers who will litigate the dispute, but it's certainly not in the best interests of your estate and your beneficiaries.

As we've seen throughout this book, estate planning is technical, and laws and procedures vary greatly from place to place. If you do it yourself, you risk making mistakes that could cost your beneficiaries. In addition, having the wrong lawyer can create future problems or add unnecessary complexity to your plan.

You may think that your wishes are "simple" and that putting them into effect is no big deal. In fact, I have had very few clients who didn't think their situation was "simple." But many times situations may appear simple only because you haven't considered the potential problems.

Let me give you a few examples to show you what I mean. These examples are not outlandish hypotheticals, but are based on actual situations:

Example #1

Mr. and Mrs. ABC want to leave everything to each other and, after the death of both of them, to their two adult children. They each prepare a Will which says something like, "I give, devise, and bequeath my entire estate to my spouse, but if my spouse is not then living, to my children in equal shares." They believe that this guarantees that upon the death of both of them, their children will receive whatever is left of their property. Seems simple enough-why do they need an estate planning attorney?

Their belief is mistaken. Whichever one of them dies first is leaving his or her property to the surviving spouse. The surviving spouse can change his or her Will and leave the property to anyone-from a second spouse to a scam artist. Without an attorney, Mr. and Mrs. ABC might not be aware of that possibility. They may still feel comfortable leaving everything to each other but, if not, an attorney can set up trusts to protect the children's inheritance.

Example #2

Mr. XYZ wants to leave everything to charity-simple, right? He prepared his own Will and did an excellent job. Why does he need an estate planning attorney?

It turns out he is disinheriting an adult child. A disinherited child might be tempted to challenge the validity of the Will in court (because if the Will is invalid, the child might inherit by intestacy). If Mr. XYZ has an attorney assist him in preparing his Will, it makes it harder to invalidate for a number of reasons.

- It eliminates the argument that the disinheritance was a mistake-the result of Mr. XYZ having prepared his own Will without the assistance of an attorney.

- Correspondence and memos in the attorney's files can be used to prove that the disinheritance was deliberate, and was done when Mr. XYZ was of sound mind.

- The attorney can advise Mr. XYZ that a better way to go would be with a revocable living trust, which could maintain his privacy and allow his assets to be distributed without notifying the disinherited child.

- In some states, if Mr. XYZ signs his Will under the supervision of an attorney, then it is presumed to have been validly executed.

Example #3

Wife is married to Husband, her second spouse. Wife has three adult children from a prior marriage. Husband has one adult child from a prior marriage. Wife goes to her lawyer and says that if Husband survives her, then she wants to leave 70% of her estate to Husband and the other 30% of her estate to her 3 children. If Husband does not survive her, then she wants her entire estate to pass to her three children.

The lawyer dutifully draws up a Will that says something like "Upon my death I give, devise, and bequeath my residuary estate 70% to Husband and 30% to my three children in equal shares." Sounds simple, right? Why does Wife need a better lawyer?

This is a disaster waiting to happen. Think about what happens if Wife dies first. Husband receives 70% of Wife's estate and each of Wife's children receives 10%. That's okay so far.

Husband later dies (perhaps as soon as the next day). Who now gets the 70% of Wife's estate that was left to him? Do Wife's children get it? No, Wife left it to Husband outright, so now it passes to his estate. As it turns out, Husband's Will leaves his entire estate to his only child.

Bottom line: Husband's child winds up with 70% of Wife's estate, while each of Wife's children gets only 10%. Is this what you think Wife wanted? Wife's estate planning attorney could have solved this problem by using a trust to benefit Husband during his lifetime, while at the same time preserving her children's inheritance.

How to Choose an Attorney

You can see how important it is to have the right attorney. Start by getting recommendations from people you know, as well as other professionals you trust, such as your accountant, financial advisor, insurance agent, or banker. You should be able to answer the following questions about any attorney that you might hire:

- Where is the attorney licensed to practice law?
- What type of law does the attorney practice and how much experience does he or she have?
- Are you comfortable discussing personal matters with the attorney?
- Is the written communication you receive from the attorney clear? Does it make sense to you?
- How will the attorney charge you for the work?

Choose an Attorney Licensed in Your Domicile

An attorney must be admitted to the bar (licensed) by each state in which he or she practices law. The state that has legal control (**jurisdiction**) over the settlement of your estate is, generally speaking, the state of your legal residence or **domicile** when you die. It's best to choose an estate planning attorney who is licensed in the state of your domicile.

A typical definition of domicile is "a fixed, permanent and principal home to which a person wherever temporarily located always intends to return." (NY SCPA §103(15); *O'Neill's Estate* v. *Tuomey Hospital*, 254 S.C. 578 (S.C. 1970)). In many cases, it's easy to determine your domicile. However, it can get complicated if you have more than one residence and/or have businesses and property in more than one state. You can have more than one residence, but you can only have one domicile.

If you're not sure which state is your domicile, discuss it with your prospective attorney. Although the definitions of domicile usually refer to a person's intention, as a practical matter some of the following factors may apply:

- How many days out of the year do you live in the state?
- Do you have a residence in the state?
- Do you own real estate in the state?
- Do you own other types of property located in the state?
- Do you file income tax returns in the state?
- Are you registered to vote in the state?
- Do you have a driver's license in the state?
- Do you own or operate a business in the state?

In addition, if you own real estate or tangible personal property in a state other than your domicile, that other state will generally have jurisdiction over that specific property. Your estate planning attorney may have to consult with, and you may have to hire, an attorney licensed in the other state in order to plan for your out-of-state property.

Choose an Estate Planning Attorney

The practice of law has become so complicated that it is now quite common for attorneys to limit the areas of the law in which they practice.

For example, the attorney who helped you buy your home might limit his or her practice to real estate matters. A real estate lawyer might further limit his or her practice to residential real estate, as opposed to commercial real estate.

A divorce lawyer might not handle DUIs. A criminal lawyer might not handle business transactions.

You are best served by choosing an attorney to plan your estate from among experienced **estate planning attorneys**, also known as **trusts & estates attorneys**. These are attorneys who spend a significant proportion (if not all) of their professional time practicing in the area of trusts & estates law. They are highly familiar with the laws and customs of the state or states where they practice when it comes to estate planning, probate and trust matters like the ones discussed in this book. They also keep up with important changes to these laws.

If you're concerned about matters like nursing home expenses or qualifying for Medicaid, you may also wish to consult an **elder law attorney**. Elder law attorneys spend a significant proportion (if not all) of their professional time in the realm of Medicaid, long-term care, nursing home, and other issues of concern to the elderly. Because they concentrate their practice in these areas, they can more easily keep up with the complexities of the laws and regulations and any changes to them.

While many estate planning attorneys have a working knowledge of how Medicaid operates, not all of them have experience in navigating the day-to-day complexities of planning for Medicaid eligibility and applying for Medicaid. If you think you may have a need in these areas, you should discuss this with your attorney or prospective attorney.

Choose an Attorney With Experience in Your State

Let's say you're considering an estate planning attorney who is licensed to practice law in the state of your domicile. You should also find out whether the prospective attorney has experience practicing trusts & estates law in that state. Having a license to practice law in a certain state and having estate planning experience there are two different things.

For example, an attorney who practices law in State A might apply for and obtain a license in State B, but that doesn't mean that he or she has experience practicing law in State B. Evaluate both the licensure and the experience of a prospective estate planning attorney before making your choice.

Evaluating Your Comfort Level

Estate planning is more than just document production. Your attorney should counsel and advise you about the best ways to accomplish your estate planning goals and objectives.

Therefore, you should feel comfortable talking with your attorney about your goals, questions, and concerns. Estate planning is complicated and you'll need to consider many details. Your attorney should be able to explain to you why the plan is structured as it is, and how it will achieve your wishes. Don't be afraid to ask questions. If you don't understand something, go back over it until you do.

Many people, consciously or subconsciously, think that if a speaker uses a lot of jargon or is otherwise incomprehensible it means that the speaker is knowledgeable. Don't fall into that trap. If a prospective attorney can't explain something in a way that makes sense to you, that is a red flag.

If you think a prospective attorney is dismissive or overbearing, or you feel uncomfortable or pressured in any way, you should not go forward.

Evaluating Written Communications

When evaluating the written work you receive from your attorney, consider the quotation at the beginning of this book. Albert Einstein said, "Everything should be made as simple as possible, but not simpler." That is a good guide. Chances are you won't understand every word of the draft Wills, trusts and other documents your attorney prepares for you, and you should not expect to. But neither should they be completely incomprehensible.

Also, the documents used in estate planning should not resemble commodities that can be purchased off the shelf. You are not just purchasing a binder full of papers (no matter how nice the binder is). I would be wary of anything that was touted as a one-size-fits-all, fill-in-the-blanks solution. Beware of documents that have blanks that are not filled in or that have schedules and attachments which are blank.

As I mentioned at the start of this book, one of the first written items you receive from your attorney will probably be an estate planning questionnaire. The questionnaire usually asks about your family, your assets and other information necessary to plan your estate successfully. It is also often your first impression of the attorney and can provide an important clue about the attorney's communications skills. Do the questions make sense to you?

Is the questionnaire laid out in a logical fashion or is it rambling and overly long? Do you get tired just looking at it? The questionnaire may tell you a lot about whether or not this attorney is someone with whom you wish to work.

About Legal Fees

Make sure you establish early on (no later than the first meeting), how the attorney will charge you for the work. While some attorneys will quote a flat fee, many attorneys charge by the hour. The hourly rate is usually a function of the attorney's experience. The more experienced the attorney, presumably the less time the work will take.

Some estate planning attorneys use paralegals and will charge you for the paralegals' time. In theory, this saves money because presumably the paralegal is performing functions (at a lower hourly rate) which the attorney would otherwise be performing (at a higher hourly rate). For example, paralegals can help to transfer property into an RLT efficiently. But beware of being charged for secretarial tasks, such as setting up meetings and the like. You may want to ask the prospective attorney about paralegal charges and listen carefully to the answers.

Keeping Your Estate Plan Up to Date

Once you have an estate plan, it's tempting to put it away and forget about it. That may be reasonable for a time. But you don't want an out-of-date estate plan to create problems for your beneficiaries. Here are some tips to help you keep your estate plan up to date and problem free.

If You Move to a Different State

What happens if you've planned your estate with the help of an attorney in one state, but later move to another? Will your estate plan still be valid? Just as important, will it still function in a way that accomplishes your goals and objectives?

If you move, the best course of action is to have a licensed, experienced estate planning attorney in your new location review your estate plan. The attorney can make sure that the documents function as intended under the law of your new state. Your estate plan may still be fine the way it is, or it may need some minor changes, or it may need to be totally re-done. Your new attorney can make recommendations and explain any necessary changes.

When Should You Review Your Estate Plan?

You should review your estate plan any time there is a significant change in your family or financial situation. You may also want to review it at set intervals, for example, every few years. Here are some situations that may prompt you to review your plan:

- you become aware of a change in federal or state law,
- you get married, divorced or re-married,
- you have a new child or grandchild,
- you wish to change who you named as executor or trustee, or your named executor or trustee dies,
- you wish to change who you named as your children's guardian or your named guardian dies,
- one of your beneficiaries dies,

- a beneficiary's situation changes (for example, marital problems, substance abuse),
- your assets change in a significant way,
- you inherit assets or receive assets as a gift,
- you purchase new or additional life insurance,
- you change your mind about the distribution of your estate, or
- you feel uneasy about any part of your estate plan.

How Should You Make Changes to Your Estate Plan?

If you think you need to make changes, contact your attorney for help. It is not enough for you simply to write your new wishes on your documents, cross things out, or send a letter to your attorney about the changes you wish to make.

All changes must be made with the appropriate legal formalities. For example, you can't change a Will by altering the document. Rather, your attorney may prepare a separate document called a codicil (an amendment to your Will), which must be signed and witnessed just like a Will. Or, because computers make it so easy these days, your attorney may prepare a new Will altogether. It's less confusing to have a new Will than an old one with many codicils.

Similarly, to change a trust, your attorney may prepare an amendment to your old trust, or may prepare a new trust agreement. A new trust document avoids the complication of a trust agreement with many separate amendments. Another advantage of a new document is that your beneficiaries won't see changes that were made with respect to property passing to them.

Your attorney can guide you in the best way to update your estate plan.

- ## *Remember*

In the complex and technical world of estate planning, what appears "simple" can cause problems down the road.

You are best off with the guidance of an estate planning attorney who is licensed and experienced in the state of your domicile.

Make sure you are comfortable with your estate planning attorney and that he or she has excellent oral and written communications skills.

Conclusion

You have a lot of choice when it comes to estate planning. You want to make sure that the money you spend on it is money well spent. How you do that starts with understanding the basic concepts and building blocks of estate planning. Next you need to find the right attorney to help you define and achieve your estate planning goals and objectives. Finally, you need the confidence to ask the right questions and the ability to evaluate the answers based on your own knowledge.

I hope this book has helped you acquire the knowledge you need to move forward confidently with your estate planning. Don't forget-You are the Savvy Client!

Index

account, 11, 48
accounting, 11, 48
advance directives, 52
agent, 46
attorney-in-fact, 46
beneficial ownership, 56
beneficiary, 9, 55
beneficiary designation, 19
bequest, 9
conservator, 36, 44
conservator of the estate, 37
created (how a trust is), 60
custodian, 37
decedent, 9
devise, 9
discretion, 61
domicile, 85
elder law attorney, 87
estate, 8
estate plan, 8
estate planning attorney, 87
executor, 11
funded (how a trust is), 60
general durable power of attorney, 47
general power of attorney, 47
grantor, 55
guardian, 36, 44
guardianship, 43
Health Care Power of Attorney, 52
incapacitated, 43

intangible personal property, 8
intestacy, 29
intestacy laws, 29
intestate estate, 29
joint owner, 44
jurisdiction, 11, 85
Last Will and Testament, 29
legal heirs, 29
legal ownership, 56
living trust, 59
Living Will, 52
non-probate property, 24
personal property, 8
personal representative, 11
pourover Will, 75
power of attorney, 46
principal, 46
probate, 11
probate estate, 9, 24
probate property, 24
property, 8
real property, 8
residuary clause, 34
residuary estate, 33
residue, 33
revocable living trust, 65
springing power of attorney, 49
surviving spouse, 9
tangible personal property, 8
taxable estate, 9
testamentary trust, 59
trust, 55
trust agreement, 60
trust document, 60

trust property, **61**
trustee, **55**

trusts & estates attorney,
87
Will, **29**

Made in the USA
San Bernardino, CA
29 September 2017